Employer Rights and Responsibilities
Following a Federal OSHA Inspection

U.S. Department of Labor

Occupational Safety and Health Administration

OSHA 3000-09R
2011

U.S. Department of Labor
Hilda L. Solis, Secretary of Labor

Contents

After a Federal OSHA Inspection

This pamphlet contains important information regarding employer rights and responsibilities following a Federal Occupational Safety and Health Administration (OSHA) inspection under the *Occupational Safety and Health Act of 1970* (OSH Act), as amended. Under the OSH Act, employers have the responsibility to provide a safe workplace.

An OSHA compliance safety and health officer (CSHO) conducts an inspection of your workplace, in accordance with the OSH Act. After the inspection, the CSHO reports the findings to the OSHA area director who evaluates them. If a violation exists, OSHA will issue you a **Citation and Notification of Penalty** detailing the exact nature of the violation(s) and any associated penalties. A citation informs you of the alleged violation, sets a proposed time period within which to correct the violation, and proposes the appropriate dollar penalties.

The information in this booklet can and should be used as a discussion guide during your closing conference with the CSHO. For each apparent violation found during the inspection, the compliance officer has discussed or will discuss the following with you:

- Nature of the violation;
- Possible abatement measures you may take to correct the violative condition;
- Possible abatement dates you may be required to meet; and
- Any penalties that the area director may issue.

The CSHO is a highly trained professional who can help you recognize and evaluate hazards as well as suggest appropriate methods of correcting violations. To minimize employee exposure to possible hazardous conditions, abatement efforts should always begin as soon as possible.

Types of Violations

The following general information defines the types of violations and explains the actions you may take if you receive a citation as the result of an inspection.

In settling a penalty, OSHA has a policy of reducing penalties for small employers and those acting in good faith.

Willful: A willful violation exists under the OSH Act where an employer has demonstrated either an intentional disregard for the requirements of the OSH Act or a plain indifference to employee safety and health. Penalties range from $5,000 to $70,000 per willful violation.

Serious: Section 17(k) of the OSH Act provides that "a serious violation shall be deemed to exist in a place of employment if there is a substantial probability that death or serious physical harm could result from a condition which exists, or from one or more practices, means, methods, operations, or processes which have been adopted or are in use, in such place of employment unless the employer did not, and could not with the exercise of reasonable diligence, know of the presence of the violation." OSHA may propose a penalty of up to $7,000 for each violation.

Other-Than-Serious: This type of violation is cited in situations where the accident/incident or illness that would be most likely to result from a hazardous condition would probably not cause death or serious physical harm, but would have a direct and immediate relationship to the safety and health of employees. OSHA may impose a penalty of up to $7,000 for each violation.

De Minimis: *De minimis* conditions are those where an employer has implemented a measure different from one specified in a standard, that has no direct or immediate relationship to safety or health. These conditions do not result in citations or penalties.

Failure to Abate: A failure to abate violation exists when a previously cited hazardous condition, practice or non-complying equipment has not been brought into compliance since the prior inspection (i.e., the violation remains continuously uncorrected) and is discovered at a later inspection. If, however, the violation was corrected, but later reoccurs, the subsequent occurrence is a repeated violation. OSHA may impose a penalty of up to $7,000 per day for each violation.

Repeated: An employer may be cited for a repeated violation if that employer has been cited previously, within the last five years, for the same or a substantially similar condition or hazard and the citation has become a final order of the Occupational Safety and Health Review Commission (OSHRC). A citation may become a final order by operation of law when an employer does not contest the citation, or pursuant to court decision or settlement. Repeated violations can bring a civil penalty of up to $70,000 for each violation.

Posting Requirements

When you receive a Citation and Notification of Penalty, you must post the citation (or a copy of it) at or near the place where each violation occurred to make employees aware of the hazards to which they may be exposed. The citation must remain posted in a place where employees can see it, for three working days or until the violation is corrected, whichever is longer. (Saturdays, Sundays, and Federal holidays are not counted as working days.) **You must comply with these posting requirements even if you contest the citation.**

The abatement certification documents – such as abatement certifications, abatement plans and progress reports – also must be posted at or near the place where the violation occurred. For moveable equipment found to be in violation and where the posting of violations would be difficult or impractical, the employer has the option to identify the equipment with a "Warning" tag specified in the abatement verification regulation, Title 29 *Code of Federal Regulations* (CFR) 1903.19(i).

Employer Options

As an employer who has been cited, you may take either of the following courses of action:

- If you agree to the Citation and Notification of Penalty, you must correct the condition by the date set in the citation and pay the penalty, if one is proposed.
- If you do not agree, you have 15 working days from the date you receive the citation to contest in writing any or all of the following:
  – Citation;

  – Proposed penalty; and/or

  – Abatement date.

Before deciding to contest the citation, you may request an informal conference with the OSHA area director within the 15 working day period to discuss any issues related to the Citation and Notification of Penalty. (See the following section on Informal Conference and Settlement).

OSHA will inform the affected employee representatives of the informal conference or contest.

Informal Conference and Settlement

Before deciding whether to file a **Notice of Intent to Contest**, you may request an informal conference with the OSHA area director to discuss the Citation and Notification of Penalty. You may use this opportunity to do any of the following:

- Obtain a better explanation of the violations cited;
- Obtain a more complete understanding of the specific standards that apply;
- Negotiate and enter into an informal settlement agreement;
- Discuss ways to correct violations;
- Discuss issues concerning proposed penalties;
- Discuss proposed abatement dates;
- Resolve disputed citations and penalties, (thereby eliminating the need for the more formal procedures associated with litigation before the Occupational Safety and Health Review Commission); and
- Obtain answers to any other questions you may have.

OSHA encourages you to take advantage of the opportunity to have an informal conference if you foresee any difficulties in complying with any part of the citation. **Please note, however, that an informal conference must be held within the 15-working-day Notice of Intent to Contest period and will neither extend the 15-working-day contest period nor take the place of the filing of a written notice if you desire to contest**. Employee representative(s) have the right to participate in any informal conference or negotiations between the regional administrator or area director and the employer.

If you agree that the cited violations exist, but you have a valid reason for wishing to extend the abatement date(s), you may discuss this with the area director in an informal conference. He or she may issue an amended citation that changes the abatement date prior to the expiration of the 15-working-day period without your filing a Notice of Intent to Contest.

If you do not contest within 15 working days, your citation will become a final order not subject to review by any court or agency. After this occurs, the OSHA area director may continue to provide you with information and assistance on how to abate the hazards cited in your citation, but may not amend or change any citation or penalty which has become a final order. The area director may only advise you on abatement methods or extend the time you need to abate the violation. (**See Petition for Modification of Abatement**).

Whenever the employer, an affected employee, or employee representative requests an informal conference, **all** the parties shall be afforded the opportunity to participate fully. If either party chooses not to participate in the informal confer-ence, that party forfeits the right to be consulted before decisions are made that affect the citations. If the requesting party objects to the attendance of the other party, OSHA may hold separate informal conferences. During a joint informal conference, separate or private discussions will be permitted if either party requests them. Informal conferences may be held by any means practical.

How to Comply

For violations you do not contest, you must:
(1) promptly notify the OSHA area director by letter, signed by a member of management, that you have taken the appropriate corrective action within the time set forth in the citation, and
(2) pay any penalties itemized.

The notification you send the area director is referred to as **Abatement Certification**. For Other-Than-Serious violations, this may be a signed letter identifying the inspection number and the citation item number and noting that you corrected the violation by the date specified on the citation. For more serious violations (such as Serious, Willful, Repeated, or Failure to Abate), abatement certification requires more detailed proof.

If the employer has abatement questions after the inspection, the area director must ensure that additional information, if available, is provided to the employer as soon as possible.

Employers also can find guidance on abatement verification on OSHA's website at www.osha.gov/Publications/Abate/abate.html.

When the citation permits an extended time for abatement, you must ensure that employees are adequately protected during this time. For example, the citation may require the immediate use of personal protective equipment by employees while engineering controls are being installed. When indicated on the citation, you must also provide OSHA with an abatement plan (steps you will take to protect employees and correct the hazards) and periodic progress reports on your actions.

The penalties itemized on the Citation and Notification of Penalty are payable within 15 working days of receipt of the penalty notice. If, however, you contest the citation or penalty in good faith, OSHA will suspend abatement and payment of penalties for those items contested until the Occupational Safety and Health Review Commission (OSHRC), or a higher court, issues a final order or decision. The OSHRC is an independent agency and is **not** a part of the U.S. Department of Labor. The final order of OSHRC will either uphold, modify, or eliminate the citations and/or penalties. Penalties for items not contested, however, are still due within 15 working days. (For further details, see the following section on **How to Contest Citations**.)

Payment should be made by check or money order payable to DOL-OSHA. Please indicate on your payment the OSHA number from the upper right-hand corner of your citation and **send it to the OSHA area office listed on the Citation and Notification of Penalty.**

How to Contest Citations

If you wish to contest any portion of your citation, you must submit a Notice of Intent to Contest in writing to the OSHA area office within 15 working days after receipt of the Citation and Notification of Penalty. This applies even if you have stated your disagreement with a citation, penalty, or abatement date during a telephone conversation or an informal conference.

The Notice of Intent to Contest must clearly state what is being contested – the citation, the penalty, the abatement date, or any combination of these factors. In addition, the notice must state whether all the violations on the citation, or just specific violations, are being contested. (For example, "I wish to contest the citation and penalty proposed for items 3 and 4 of the citation issued June 27, 2011").

Your contest must be made in good faith. OSHA will not consider a contest filed solely to avoid your responsibilities for abatement or payment of penalties.

A proper contest of any item suspends your legal obligation to abate and pay until the item contested has been resolved. If you contest only the dates indicated on the citation or if you contest only some items on the citation, you must correct the other items by the abatement date and pay the corresponding penalties within 15 days of notification.

After you file a Notice of Intent to Contest, your case is officially in litigation. If you wish to settle the case, you may contact the OSHA area director who will give you the name of the attorney handling your case for OSHA. All settlements of contested cases are negotiated between you and the attorney according to the rules of procedure of the OSHRC.

The Contest Process

If you file the written Notice of Intent to Contest within the required 15 working days, the OSHA area director forwards your case to the OSHRC. The OSHRC hears employer contests of OSHA citations. They are an independent agency separate from the Department of Labor. The OSHRC assigns the case to an administrative law judge who usually will schedule a hearing in a public place close to your workplace. Both employers and employees have the right to participate in this hearing, which contains all the elements of a trial, including examination and cross-examination of witnesses. You may choose to represent yourself or have an attorney represent you. The administrative law judge may affirm, modify, or eliminate any contested items of the citation or penalty.

As with any other legal procedure, there is an appeals process. Once the administrative law judge has ruled, any party to the case may request a further review by the full OSHRC. In addition, any of the three commissioners may, on his or her own motion, bring the case before the entire OSHRC for review. The OSHRC's ruling, in turn, may be appealed to the Federal circuit court in which the case arose or for the Federal circuit where the employer has his or her principal office.

For more information, write to:

U.S. Occupational Safety and Health
Review Commission
1120 20th Street NW, 9th Floor
Washington, DC 20036
Phone: 202-606-5400 Fax: 202-606-5050
www.oshrc.gov

Petition for Modification of Abatement

OSHA assigns abatement dates on the basis of the best information available when issuing the citation. If you are unable to meet an abatement date because of uncontrollable events or other circumstances, and the 15-working-day contest period has expired, you may file a **Petition for Modification of Abatement** (PMA) with the OSHA area director.

The petition must be in writing and must be submitted as soon as possible, **but no later than one working day after the abatement date**. To show clearly that you have made a good-faith effort to comply, the PMA must include all of the following information before OSHA considers it:

- Steps you have taken to achieve compliance, and dates they were taken;
- Additional time you need to comply;
- Why you need additional time;
- Interim steps you are taking to safeguard your employees against the cited hazard(s) until the abatement; and
- A certification that the petition has been posted, the date of posting and, when appropriate, a statement that the petition has been furnished to an authorized representative of the affected employees. The petition must remain posted for 10 working days, during which employees may file an objection.

The OSHA area director may grant or oppose a PMA. If it is opposed, it automatically becomes a contested case before the OSHRC. If a PMA is granted, OSHA may conduct a monitoring inspection to ensure that conditions are as they have been described and that adequate progress has been made toward abatement. The OSHA area office may provide additional information on PMAs.

What Employees Can Do

Employees or their authorized representatives may contest any or all of the abatement dates set for violations if they believe them to be unreasonable. A written Notice of Intent to Contest must be filed with the OSHA area director within 15 working days after the employer receives the citation.

The filing of an employee contest does not suspend the employer's obligation to abate.

Employees also have the right to object to a PMA. Such objections must be in writing and must be sent to the area office within 10 days of service or posting. OSHA will not make a decision regarding the PMA until the Review Commission resolves the issue.

Follow-up Inspections and Failure to Abate

If you receive a citation, a follow-up inspection may be conducted to verify that you have done the following:

- Posted the citation as required,
- Corrected the violations as required in the citation, and/or
- Protected employees adequately and made appropriate progress in correcting hazards during multistep or lengthy abatement periods.

In addition to providing for penalties for failure-to-post citations and failure-to-abate violations, the OSH Act clearly states that you have a **continuing responsibility** to comply with the OSH Act and assure your employees safe and healthful working conditions. OSHA will cite any new violations discovered during a follow-up inspection.

Employer Responsibilities

Employers have the responsibility to provide a safe workplace. Employers MUST provide their employees with a workplace that does not have serious hazards and must follow all OSHA safety and health standards. Employers must find and correct safety and health problems.

Employers MUST also:

- Inform employees about hazards through training, labels, alarms, color-coded systems, chemical information sheets and other methods.
- Train employees in a language and vocabulary they can understand.
- Keep accurate records of work-related injuries and illnesses.
- Perform tests in the workplace, such as air sampling, required by some OSHA standards.
- Provide hearing exams or other medical tests required by OSHA standards.
- Post OSHA citations and injury and illness data where workers can see them.
- Notify OSHA within eight hours of a workplace fatality or when three or more workers are hospitalized.
- Prominently display the official OSHA poster that describes rights and responsibilities under the OSH Act.

Employee Discrimination

Section 11(c) of the OSH Act prohibits employers from discharging or otherwise discriminating against an employee who has exercised any right under this law, including the right to make safety and health complaints or to request an OSHA inspection. OSHA will investigate complaints from employees who believe they have been discriminated against. If the investigation discloses probable violations of employee rights, court action may follow.

Employees who believe they have been discriminated against must file their complaints within **30 days** of the alleged act of discrimination. For more information, contact OSHA at www.osha.gov or call 1-800-321-OSHA (6742). In states with OSHA-approved state programs, an employee who believes he/she has been discriminated against under Section 11(c) of the OSH Act is entitled to file a complaint alleging discrimination under both state and federal procedures.

Providing False Information

All information employers report to OSHA must be accurate and truthful. Providing false information on efforts to abate cited conditions or in required records is punishable under the OSH Act.

OSHA Assistance, Services and Programs

OSHA can provide extensive help through a variety of programs, including free workplace consultations, compliance assistance, voluntary protection programs, strategic partnerships, alliances, and training and education. For more information on any of the programs listed below, visit OSHA's website at www.osha.gov or call 1-800-321-OSHA (6742).

Establishing an Injury and Illness Prevention Program

The key to a safe and healthful work environment is a comprehensive injury and illness prevention program.

Injury and illness prevention programs, known by a variety of names, are universal interventions that can substantially reduce the number and severity of workplace injuries and alleviate the associated financial burdens on U.S. workplaces. Many states have requirements or voluntary guidelines for workplace injury and illness prevention programs. Also, numerous employers in the United States already manage safety using injury and illness prevention programs, and we believe that all employers can and should do the same. Most successful injury and illness prevention programs are based on a common set of key elements. These include management leadership, worker participation, hazard identification, hazard prevention and control, education and training, and program evaluation and improvement. Visit OSHA's website at http://www.osha.gov/dsg/topics/safetyhealth/index.html for more information and guidance on establishing effective injury and illness prevention programs in the workplace.

Compliance Assistance Specialists

OSHA has compliance assistance specialists throughout the nation who can provide information and assistance to employers and workers. There is generally at least one compliance assistance specialist in each area office in states under Federal OSHA jurisdiction. They respond to requests for help from a variety of groups including small businesses, trade associations, local unions, and community and faith-based organizations. Compliance assistance specialists provide technical assistance, information on OSHA standards, seminars or workshops, and information on OSHA's educational and training resources. Contact your local OSHA office for more information.

OSHA's Free On-site Consultation Service for Small Employers

OSHA's On-site Consultation Program offers free and confidential advice to small and medium-sized businesses in all states across the country, with priority given to high-hazard worksites.

On-site Consultation services are separate from enforcement and do not result in penalties or citations. Consultants from state agencies or universities work with employers to identify workplace hazards, provide advice on compliance with OSHA standards, and assist in establishing injury and illness prevention programs.

In FY 2010, responding to requests from small employers looking to create or improve their injury and illness prevention programs, OSHA's On-site Consultation Program conducted over 30,000 visits to small business worksites covering over 1.5 million workers across the nation.

To request such services, an employer can phone or write to the OSHA Consultation Program. See the Small Business section of OSHA's website for contact information for the consultation offices in every state (www.osha.gov/dcsp/smallbusiness/index.html) or call 1-800-321-OSHA (6742).

- **Safety and Health Achievement Recognition Program**
  Under the consultation program, certain exemplary employers may request participation in OSHA's Safety and Health Achievement Recognition Program (SHARP). Eligibility for participation includes, but is not limited to, receiving a full-service, comprehensive consultation visit, correcting all identified hazards, and developing an effective injury and illness prevention program.

Cooperative Programs

OSHA offers cooperative programs to help prevent fatalities, injuries and illnesses in the workplace.

- **Alliance Program**

  Through the Alliance Program, OSHA works with groups committed to worker safety and health to prevent workplace fatalities, injuries and illnesses. These groups include businesses, trade or professional organizations, unions, consulates, faith- and community-based organizations, and educational institutions. OSHA and the groups work together to develop compliance assistance tools and resources, share information with workers and employers, and educate workers and employers about their rights and responsibilities.

- **Challenge Program**

  This program helps employers and workers improve their safety and health management systems and implement an effective system to prevent fatalities, injuries and illnesses.

- **OSHA Strategic Partnership Program (OSPP)**

  Partnerships are formalized through tailored agreements designed to encourage, assist and recognize partner efforts to eliminate serious hazards and achieve model workplace safety and health practices.

- **Voluntary Protection Programs (VPP)**

  The VPP recognize employers and workers in private industry and federal agencies who have implemented effective safety and health management systems and maintain injury and illness rates below national Bureau of Labor Statistics averages for their respective industries. In VPP, management, labor and OSHA work cooperatively and proactively to prevent fatalities, injuries and illnesses.

OSHA Training Institute Education Centers

The OSHA Training Institute (OTI) Education Centers are a national network of nonprofit organizations authorized by OSHA to conduct occupational safety and health training to private sector workers, supervisors and employers.

Susan Harwood Training and Education Grants

OSHA provides grants to nonprofit organizations to provide worker education and training on serious job hazards and avoidance/prevention strategies.

Information and Publications

OSHA has a variety of educational materials and electronic tools available on its website at www.osha.gov. These include Safety and Health Topics Pages, Safety Fact Sheets, Expert Advisor software, copies of regulations and compliance directives, videos and other information for employers and workers.

In addition, OSHA has available extensive publications to help explain OSHA standards, job hazards, and mitigation strategies and provide assistance in developing effective safety and health programs.

For a listing of free publications, visit OSHA's website at www.osha.gov or call 1-800-321-OSHA (6742).

QuickTakes

OSHA's free, twice-monthly online newsletter, QuickTakes, offers the latest news about OSHA initiatives and products to assist employers and workers in finding and preventing workplace hazards. To sign up for QuickTakes, visit OSHA's website at www.osha.gov and click on QuickTakes at the top of the page.

Contacting OSHA

To order additional copies of this publication,
to get a list of other OSHA publications, to ask
questions or to get more information about
OSHA's free consultation service, contact OSHA at
1-800-321-OSHA (6742), (TTY) 1-877-889-5627 or
visit www.osha.gov.

For assistance, contact us.
We are OSHA. We can help.

OSHA Regional Offices

Region I
Boston Regional Office
(CT*, ME, MA, NH, RI, VT*)
JFK Federal Building, Room E340
Boston, MA 02203
(617) 565-9860 (617) 565-9827 Fax

Region II
New York Regional Office
(NJ*, NY*, PR*, VI*)
201 Varick Street, Room 670
New York, NY 10014
(212) 337-2378 (212) 337-2371 Fax

Region III
Philadelphia Regional Office
(DE, DC, MD*, PA, VA*, WV)
The Curtis Center
170 S. Independence Mall West
Suite 740 West
Philadelphia, PA 19106-3309
(215) 861-4900 (215) 861-4904 Fax

Region IV
Atlanta Regional Office
(AL, FL, GA, KY*, MS, NC*, SC*, TN*)
61 Forsyth Street, SW, Room 6T50
Atlanta, GA 30303
(678) 237-0400 (678) 237-0447 Fax

Region V
Chicago Regional Office
(IL*, IN*, MI*, MN*, OH, WI)
230 South Dearborn Street
Room 3244
Chicago, IL 60604
(312) 353-2220 (312) 353-7774 Fax

Region VI
Dallas Regional Office
(AR, LA, NM*, OK, TX)
525 Griffin Street, Room 602
Dallas, TX 75202
(972) 850-4145 (972) 850-4149 Fax
(972) 850-4150 FSO Fax

Region VII
Kansas City Regional Office
(IA*, KS, MO, NE)
Two Pershing Square Building
2300 Main Street, Suite 1010
Kansas City, MO 64108-2416
(816) 283-8745 (816) 283-0547 Fax

Region VIII
Denver Regional Office
(CO, MT, ND, SD, UT*, WY*)
1999 Broadway, Suite 1690
Denver, CO 80202-5716
(720) 264-6550 (720) 264-6585 Fax

Region IX
San Francisco Regional Office
(AZ*, CA*, HI*, NV*, and American Samoa,
Guam and the Northern Mariana Islands)
90 7th Street, Suite 18100
San Francisco, CA 94103
(415) 625-2547 (415) 625-2534 Fax

Region X
Seattle Regional Office
(AK*, ID, OR*, WA*)
1111 Third Avenue, Suite 715
Seattle, WA 98101-3212
(206) 553-5930 (206) 553-6499 Fax

*These states and territories operate their own
OSHA-approved job safety and health plans and
cover state and local government employees as well
as private sector employees. The Connecticut, Illinois,
New Jersey, New York and Virgin Islands programs
cover public employees only. (Private sector workers
in these states are covered by Federal OSHA). States
with approved programs must have standards that
are identical to, or at least as effective as, the Federal
OSHA standards.

Note: To get contact information for OSHA area
offices, OSHA-approved state plans and OSHA
consultation projects, please visit us online at
www.osha.gov or call us at 1-800-321-OSHA (6742).

Appendix: The Small Business Regulatory Enforcement Fairness Act of 1996 (SBREFA)

In 1996, Congress passed the Small Business Regulatory Enforcement Fairness Act, or SBREFA, in response to concerns expressed by the small business community that Federal regulations were too numerous, too complex and too expensive to implement. SBREFA was designed to give small businesses assistance in understanding and complying with regulations and more of a voice in the development of new regulations. Under SBREFA, the Occupational Safety and Health Administration (OSHA) and other Federal agencies must:

- Produce Small Entity Compliance Guides for some rules;

- Be responsive to small business inquiries about compliance with the agency's regulations;

- Submit final rules to Congress for review;

- Have a penalty reduction policy for small businesses; and

- Involve small businesses in the development of some proposed rules through Small Business Advocacy Review Panels.

Commenting on Enforcement Actions

Under a law passed by Congress in 1996, the Small Business Administration (SBA) has established an SBA Ombudsman and SBA Regional Fairness Boards to investigate small business complaints about Federal agency enforcement actions.

If you are a small business and believe that you have been treated unfairly by OSHA, you may file an electronic comment/complaint with the SBA Ombudsman over the Internet at: http://www.sba.gov/ombudsman/comments/ commentform1.html

Or you may contact the SBA's Office of the National Ombudsman by:

- Toll-free Phone: (888) REG-FAIR (734-3247)
- Fax: (202) 481-5719
- E-mail: ombudsman@sba.gov
- Mail: Office of the National Ombudsman
  U.S. Small Business Administration
  409 3rd Street, S.W., MC2120
  Washington, DC 20416-0005

To view the SBREFA Act in its entirety, please visit the following web link:
http://www.sba.gov/advo/laws/sbrefa.html

For more information on SBREFA, the following web links may prove helpful:

http://www.sba.gov/ombudsman/

http://www.sba.gov/ombudsman/dsp_overview.html

http://www.sba.gov/ombudsman/dsp_faq.html

http://www.sba.gov/advo/

http://www.sba.gov/advo/laws/is_oshapanel.html

NOTE: Filing a complaint with the SBA Ombudsman does not affect any obligation that you may have to comply with an OSHA citation or other enforcement action. Nor does it mean that you need not take other available legal steps to protect your interests.